W0018881

What Are You Doing?

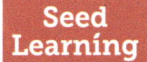

Seed Learning

playing

drinking

eating

reading

writing

drawing

studying

sleeping

What are you doing?

I'm reading a book.

What are you doing?

I'm writing a card.

What are you doing?

I'm drawing a cat.

What are you doing?

I'm eating chicken.

What are you doing?

I'm drinking orange juice.

What are you doing?

I'm sleeping.

Let's learn about Spain.

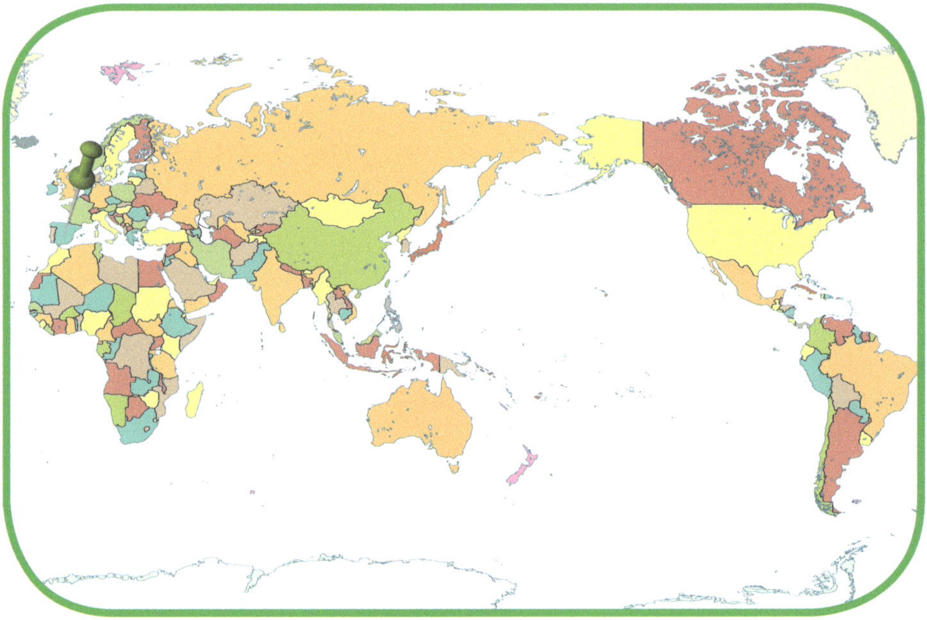

Flag of Spain

Churros